P.S.- I made this...™

I SEE IT. I LIKE IT. I MAKE IT.

Erica Domesek

Abrams Image, New York

for my Mom...
who gave me the tools for life

P.S.-I made this...™

CONTENTS

P.S.-I like to make things!
6

my tools
8

jewelry
12

accessories
76

apparel
144

P.S.-

P.S.-I like to make things!

It's no secret that I live for arts and crafts, fashion, and all things "design." With a lineage that includes Jacqueline Onassis's favored dress designer Gustave Tassell (he is my cousin) and World War II–sportswear fashions (my grandfather's sportswear company made sweaters for the US Army), I like to think I was born with DIY in my DNA.

My first fashion DIY project was inspired by an early 1980s Betsey Johnson party dress of my mother's. With some spare fabric and a few stitches, I added a ruched skirt to the bottom of a Hanes T-shirt, creating a whimsical, sweet minidress that received rave reviews.

Since a young age, my motto has been "I see it. I like it. I make it." Having spent years behind the scenes as a prop stylist and creative consultant, I've had access to the most talented people, unique places, and beautiful things. Crafting a career built on creativity has me constantly looking for inspiration everywhere, from the runways to nature to everyday objects.

I live for fashion. Like most style addicts, I lean toward those pricey designer pieces that exceed my personal budget. But one can't always drop a serious wad of cash on a clutch or a crazy-cool pair of heels. It's important to remember that trends come and go. We all crave immediate gratification, but this season's hot number will more than likely be extinct by next. My advice is to take notes about what draws you to a spectacular item and to recognize the accessible and affordable materials within it. Where can you find them? Can you paint, embellish, cut, add to, or adorn something similar to get the look and feel you've just fallen for—without breaking the bank?

Making things can be really easy and take a lot less time and energy than you expect. Think of this book as the CliffsNotes to fast fashion, with a "tongue in chic" angle. Taking risks and shortcuts are okay as long as you approach them with integrity and a bit of effort.

Peek inside your existing wardrobe to find items that are "DIY-ing" for a reinvention; give them an entirely new life, one that reflects your personality and style. Don't buy an abundance of tools and materials—chances are you probably have what you need in your junk drawer! Having a few necessary tools, such as a sharp pair of scissors, a glue gun, and a needle and thread, is just about all you need to get started. As you get deeper into your projects, build your tool box and craft kit with trips to the hardware, craft-supply, and ribbon-and-trim stores. Strolling down the aisles, even when you don't have a particular project in mind, is a great way to dream up new ideas. Or gather friends together for a DIY "crafternoon" and swap gossip over grommets and glue guns.

My most important piece of advice is to seek inspiration every day and everywhere: Scour the runways and the "real ways." Tap into your inner artist, and take notes from your design crushes. Between the sea of fantastic fashion and design magazines, online resources, and objects that stop you in your tracks, your idea handbag will be bursting at the seams.

In a world where trends are expensive and pass quickly, wouldn't you like to say, "P.S.—I made this . . ."?

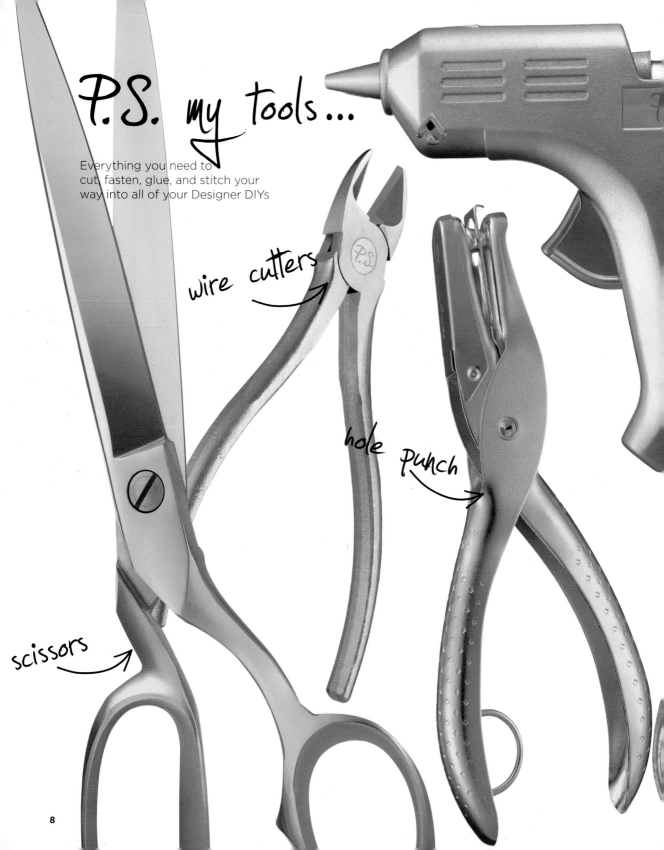

P.S. my tools...

Everything you need to
cut, fasten, glue, and stitch your
way into all of your Designer DIYs

wire cutters

hole punch

scissors

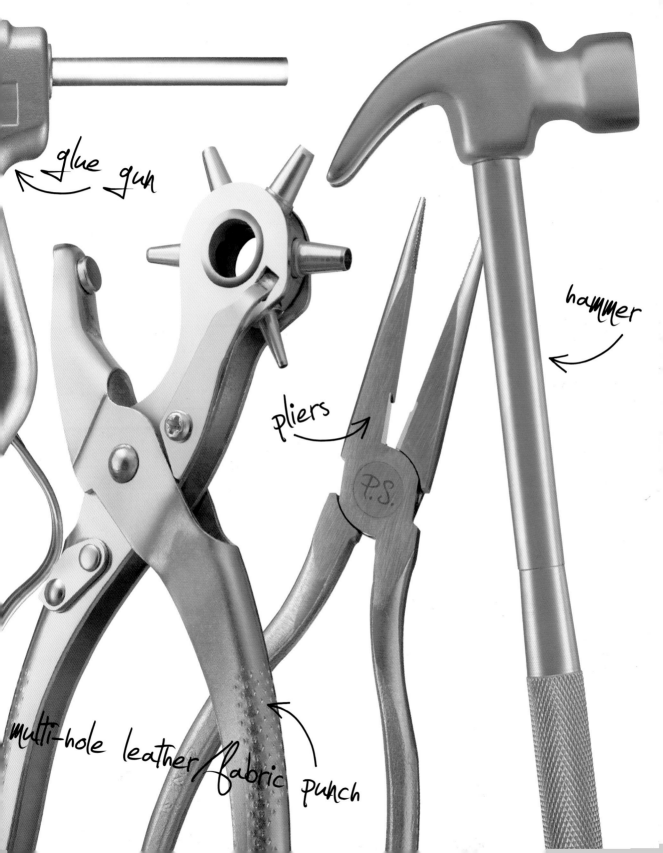

glue gun

hammer

pliers

P.S.

multi-hole leather/fabric punch

P.S.- my other tools...

sharpie

needle 'n thread

safety pins

double-sided tape

tape measure

metal clips

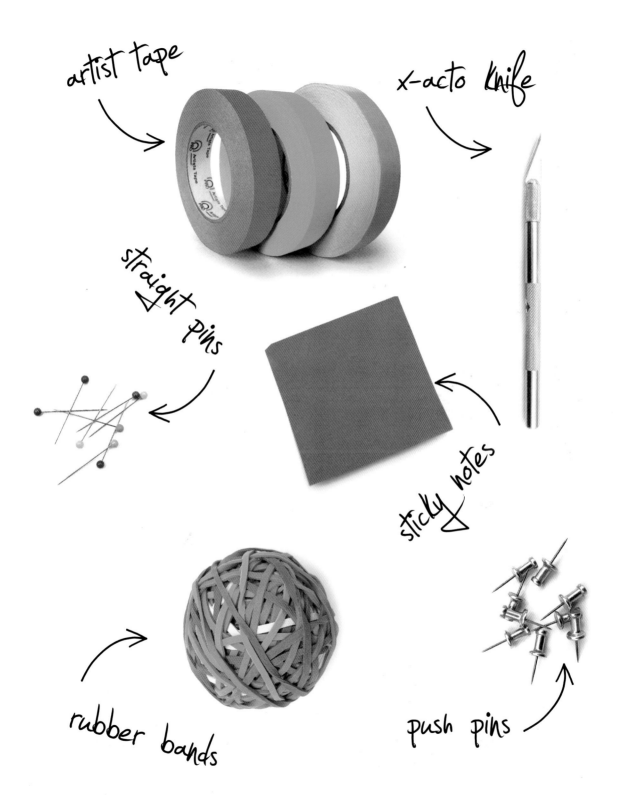

artist tape

x-acto knife

straight pins

sticky notes

rubber bands

push pins

P.S.- I made this...

JEWELRY

big ball necklace

JEWELRY

While the world may not revolve around you, we are all spinning together on a giant sphere that's orbiting the sun.

The word *sphere* hails from the Greek *sphaira*, which means globe or ball. Its round and immaculate silhouette, and perfect circular formation, lends it to symmetrical art, fashion, and everyday masterpieces.

Everyone should round out their world with 360 degrees of decadence. Don't forget to stop, breathe, and look up for heavenly globe pendant lamps and bulbous balloons, which are sure to make you smile. Find pleasure in everyday ball-like items turned into bold baubles by combining a playful profile from everyone's favorite bouncy toy with a sheer touch of style. Gather together colorful round ingredients to create an out-of-this-world accessory.

big ball necklace

JEWELRY

INGREDIENTS

- scissors
- stockings
- bouncy balls

1. Grab a pair of sheer stockings and cut off the legs. Leave room at both ends (so you can tie your necklace together when it's done).

2. Knot one leg (leave a little room at the end) and drop in bouncy balls, one at a time, tying knots between them as you go.

3. Repeat the process with the second stocking leg. Make sure that one leg has more balls. This will serve as the bottom strand.

4. Attach the legs together by knotting them. P.S.-Get creative by mixing balls of different colors and sizes with a variety of textured stockings and tights. The possibilities are endless.

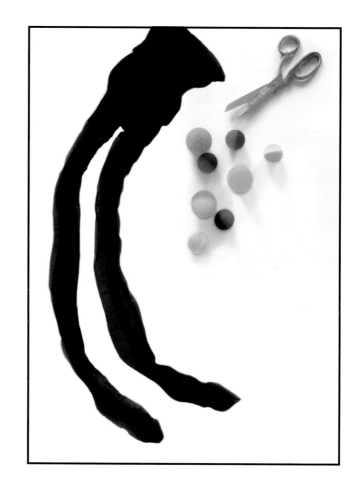

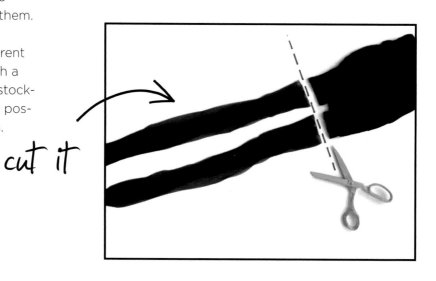

cut it

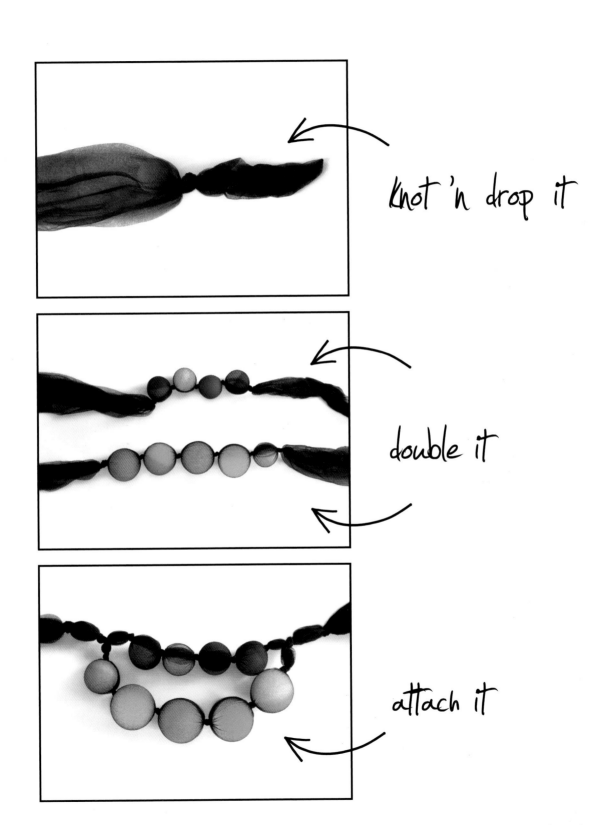

knot 'n drop it

double it

attach it

have a ball!

18

Remember days at camp spent choosing colorful embroidery threads and weaving them into bracelets for your new best friend to wear?

Fear not, friendship bracelets, we haven't forgotten you! We just have some partners in crime we'd like you to meet. As I always say, "The more the merrier," and this stackable suggestion may be worked into whatever you have in your current wrist wardrobe.

Brace yourself for a vivid mass of arm candy, one that combines bright and brilliant tones. Madonna, the innovative pop icon, was one of the first to rock an abundance of bracelets. Follow in Madge's footsteps and look to the runways for more circular repetition. Herve Leger's bandage minidresses take bondage in a new direction—and to the next level. Towers of color keep things organized and streamlined. Take note, and apply this ritual to your books, towels, and colorful tapes. A simple stack integrates high design into your everyday life. Create your own cohesive color story each season with a personal wrist palette. Push your love over the borderline: Craft a bunch of bright bangles!

bright bangles

JEWELRY

INGREDIENTS

- pipe clamps
- bright ribbons
- scissors

1. Take a trip to a magical spot where all things glitter and shine—your local hardware store! Head straight for the plumbing aisle and pick up a bunch of pipe clamps.

2. Use a screwdriver to size your bangles. Determine how loose or tight a look you want by adjusting the screws on the sides.

3. Loop your ribbon and wrap it around the bangle.

4. Once it's covered, knot it at the end. Snip remaining ribbon.

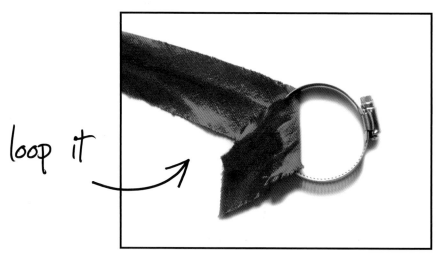

loop it

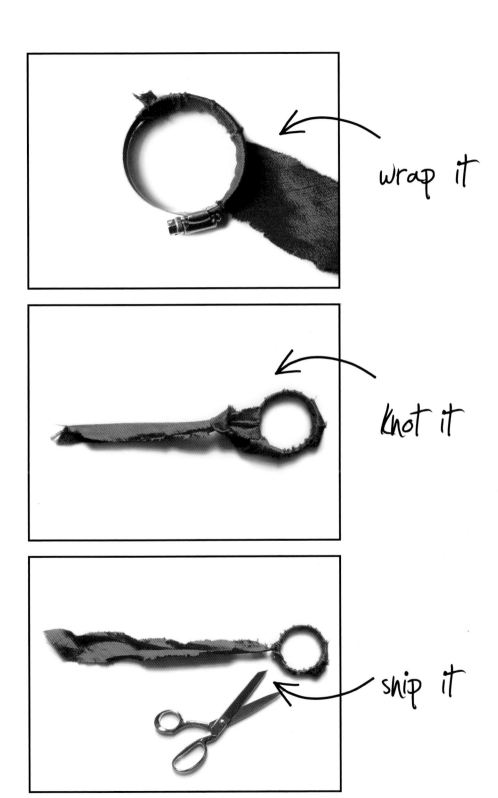

wrap it

knot it

snip it

wrap 'em 'n stack 'em!

Most amazing ideas grow from the ground up. Case in point: cane.

This earthy material is actually the hollow, jointed stem of a woody plant, most commonly rattan, which grows in South America. Once treated, it is used in wickerwork, to make chairs and other furniture.

First introduced in England toward the end of the seventeenth century, wicker has evolved in recent years, as new, intricate designs have made their way from living rooms to dressing rooms. The light-brown material has furthermore crossed over into accessories that we like to rock in beautiful and balmy climates.

The list of designers who call upon this gift from Mother Earth goes on for miles: Dior does hats, Dries Van Noten knows heels, Issey Miyake makes jewelry, Kate Spade carries handbags, and Ports 1961 has perfected belts and bags. A classic, seasonal trend, cane accessories are worn in the Hamptons and on the Cape, feted on the French Riviera, and exposed on the Amalfi coast. Whether you're looking for sun protection or simply need a touch of tan and texture, stick with cane—the look is insane!

JEWELRY

INGREDIENTS

- cane material
- bottle caps
- twist ties
- sharpie
- earring wires
- scissors

1. Buy cane material from your favorite fabric or hardware store (for the synthetic version of the material).

2. Use two different sized bottlecaps to trace, then cut out circles.

3. Color the twist tie with a Sharpie in the accent color of your choice.

4. Slide the twist tie through both circles and fold down to attach.

5. Slip on the earring wire at the top.

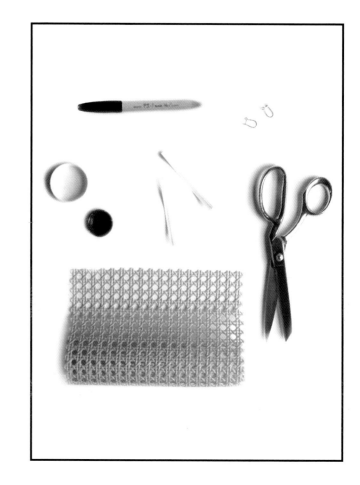

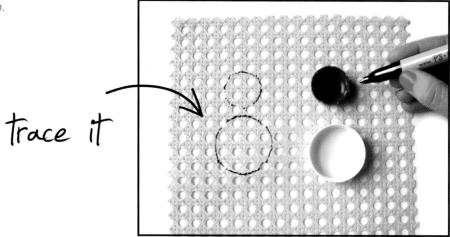

trace it

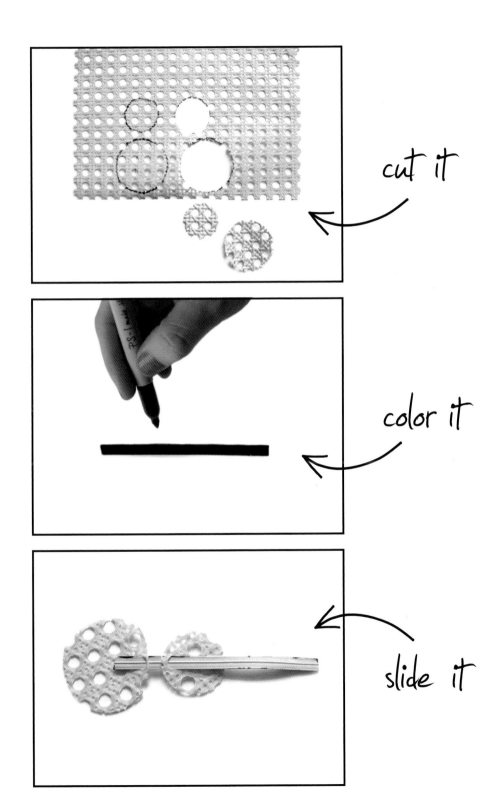

cut it

color it

slide it

snip it

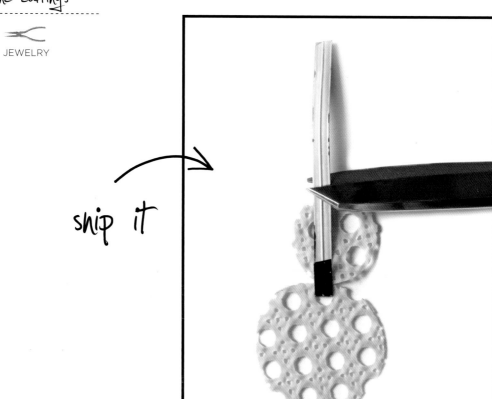

fold it

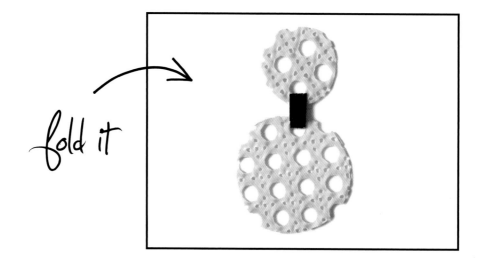

cocktail ring

JEWELRY

Go big or stay home. When it comes to cocktail rings, the bigger, the bolder, the better!

Seen on the fabulous fingers of socialites and celebrities, cocktail rings made their debut in the 1920s at Prohibition parties. When you think of over-the-top encrusted rings, a certain Ms. Taylor and the trinkets she accumulated from her collection of husbands come to mind. The cocktail ring became a noted status symbol as women wanted to drip and dazzle with diamonds, pearls, and precious gemstones.

Donning an oversized bit of bling says a lot about your personality: You—like the ring—are fearless, bold, full of sparkle and shine, and loved and cherished by many. Don't be afraid to stack and spread multiple rings on one hand. Scour flea markets and your mother's jewelry box for inspiration, and you'll find charming, chunky delights to adorn your ready-and-waiting fingers. Create an eye-catching cocktail ring by adding an oversized clip-on earring to a hair elastic.

JEWELRY

INGREDIENTS

- hair elastic
- clip-on earring
- needle 'n thread

1. Knot the hair elastic in the center.

2. Fold the hair elastic in half and clip on the earring.

3. Use a needle and thread to secure your bling to its setting.

P.S.-For a more dramatic effect, use a pair of earrings, or mix 'n match for a bold statement.

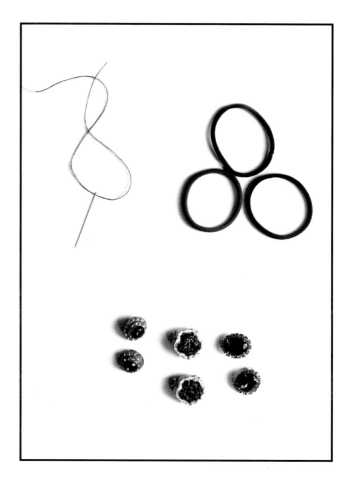

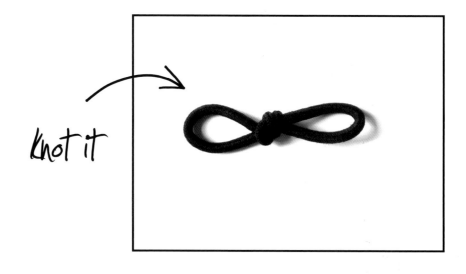

Knot it

clip it

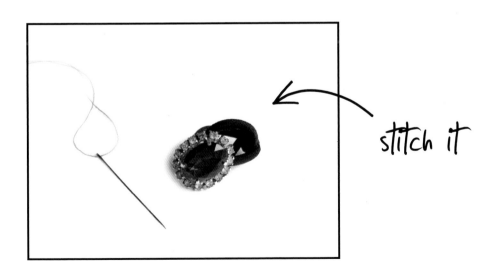

stitch it

cocktail ring
- -

JEWELRY

put a ring on it!

tribal necklace

JEWELRY

Going global is necessary when searching for an innovative style that's uniquely your own.

By borrowing from different cultures, you can create an eclectic, here-nor-there look. Enter Africa, a continent that revolutionized the blending of strong colors, vivid prints, and varied textures inspired by elements in nature and old-world tribal identities.

Striking tribal themes have frequented the runways and "real ways," where bright, beaded fabrics with graphic markings are incorporated in clothing and accessories. Intricate handwoven baskets, beaded bangles, and rich, stackable neckwear have their origins in the African homeland, as well. Supermodel and singer Grace Jones's towering presence purrs with tribal chic, while fashion's cult leaders and world travelers, such as Diane von Furstenberg, Marc Jacobs, and Oscar de la Renta, intertwine aboriginal originality and modern sensibility to create their contemporary must-haves.

Make a stunning statement day or night with your native neckwear. Mark your territory with a tribal necklace by combining a piece of beaded trim—available at any fabric, interior, or upholstery store—with bright ribbon.

tribal necklace

JEWELRY

INGREDIENTS

• beaded trim
• ribbon
• scissors
• needle 'n thread

1. Cut the trim to the desired length.

2. Cut ribbon in half. Double-knot each ribbon to one end of the trim. Snip off the ends near the knots.

3. Stitch through knots onto trim to reinforce.

4. Tie it off.

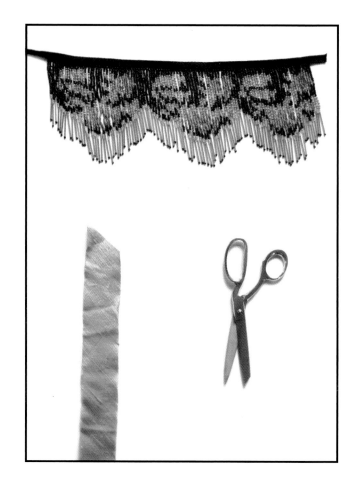

knot it

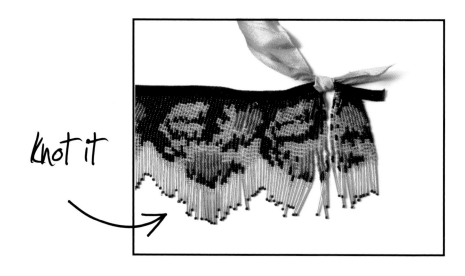

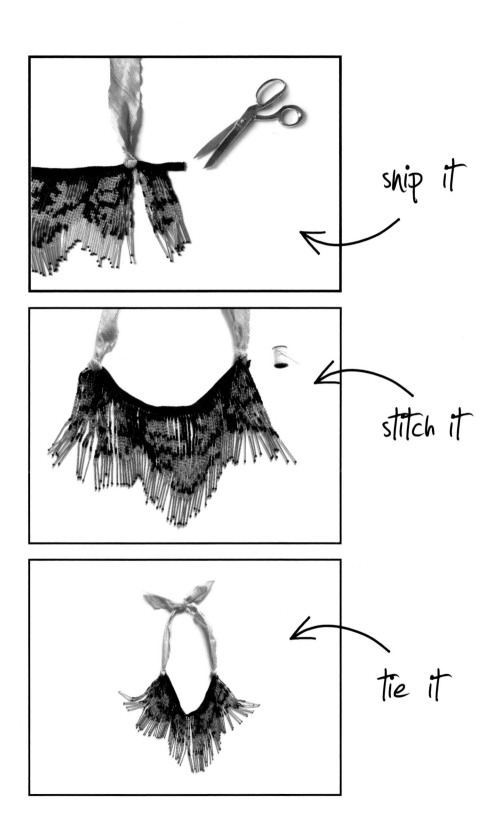

snip it

stitch it

tie it

JEWELRY

join the tribe!

Military-inspired fashions pay homage to our home-grown heroes. During World War II, the elite army units issued uniforms that were monochromatic from head to toe.

To show rank, head officers wore special embellishments, such as gold buttons, tassels, and pristine rope coils.

Fashion front lines can be intimidating; it's the details that will set you apart and let others know that you're a leader of style. The military-uniform look was adopted by civilians during the Vietnam War era, when wearing army jackets and combat boots became not only a political statement but also a fashion statement.

Balmain, Moschino, Tory Burch, and Marc Jacobs know how to keep it in line while nodding to the infantry. Stomp straight from boot camp into a fashion fortress. Implement military details in your wardrobe to create a chicly accessorized regiment. Tell people you care about your country by coveting couture. Award yourself—and your ears—with two honorary badges of effortless honor. After all, fashion is all about being "at ease" with yourself and your expression of style.

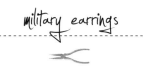

INGREDIENTS

- satin cord
- tassels
- buttons
- chain
- earring wires
- glue gun
- scissors
- wire cutters
- ribbon

1. Start by tightly coiling and gluing a thin satin cord into a flat, circular base.

2. Slip on a tassel and continue wrapping to desired earring size.

3. Create a loop at the top. Glue and trim.

4. Glue a button onto the center of the loop.

5. For a more finished look, cut and glue a piece of ribbon to the back of the loop.

6. Cut and stitch the chain.

7. Add the earring wire.

coil 'n glue it

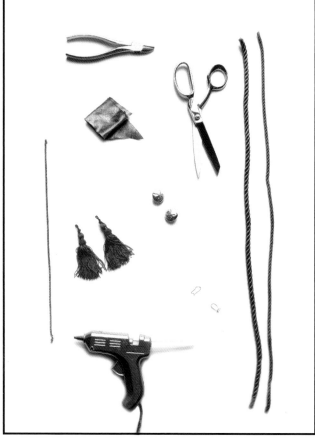

slip it

loop it

glue it

button it

cut it

glue it

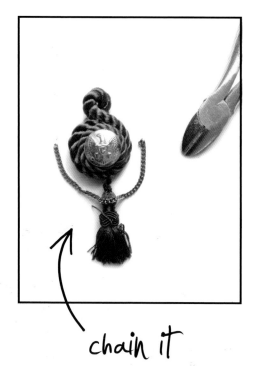

chain it

stitch it

stud cuff

JEWELRY

Age-old question: If you had to eat the same one meal every day for the rest of your life, what would it be? Answer: A big bowl of style soup!

Start with one part street chic, stir in two parts ultra edginess, sprinkle the mixture with metallic toppings, chill, and serve. My recipe: Take chances, mix in bold accents for a touch of danger, and enter the world for all to see.

Thrill seeking and risk taking make style all the more fun, especially when it comes to accessorizing. Rock 'n roll–wild children and downtown hipsters alike embrace wickedly chic wardrobes, in which basic black is turned into a bad black that's oh so good.

The bold biker trend may be a bit hardcore for some, but luxury go-to mavens, such as Hermès, Givenchy, Tory Burch, and Michael Kors, can't live without the shiny studs that spike up everyone's fashion game. The mixed-media combo of metallic studs and midnight-ebony shades is as stylish as it is strong. Be the leader of your fashion pack when you merge the street-chic cachet of a wide-cuff bracelet with your wardrobe. After all, who doesn't want some studs in their life?

stud cuff

JEWELRY

INGREDIENTS
- cardboard mailing tube
- lace
- studs
- scissors
- glue gun
- pliers

1. Cut a mailing tube horizontally to your desired cuff width.

2. Slit the mailing tube vertically to create an opening.

3. Adhere the lace to the inside of the tube with a few dots of glue.

4. Wrap the bracelet with lace.

5. Stud it up—use pliers to help reinforce the studs.

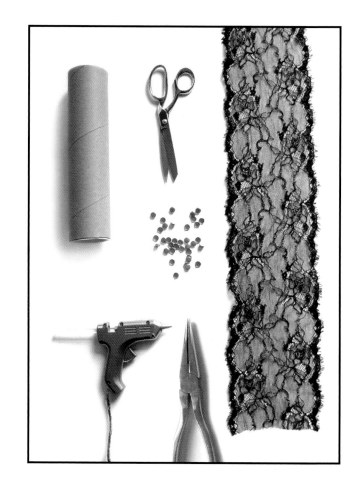

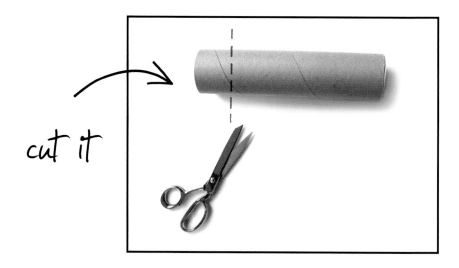

cut it

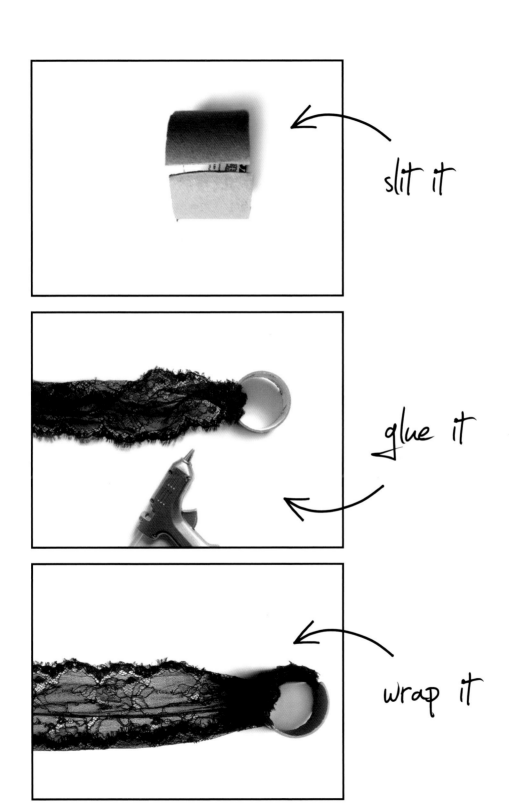

slit it

glue it

wrap it

stud it

press it

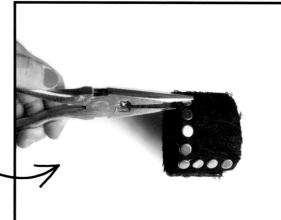

P.S.-i love hot studs!

"Raindrops on roses and whiskers on kittens" are a few of my favorite things.

Truth be told, I have so many favorite things, I suffer from an acute case of "pack rat-itus." Shadow boxes and shelves were invented to showcase your treasures, but what happens when you have more finger ornaments than fingers? If you have a collection of amazing rings 'n things, I suggest you stack 'em on a string! A stockpile of fabulous finds from over the years was hard to show off . . . until now.

Being inventive and finding different ways to wear accessories will unveil your uniqueness and set you apart. Round up your class ring, mood ring, promise ring, signet ring, cocktail ring, and anything else that's stringable and stackable, and sport them around your neck. All that sparkles and shines should rest just above your décolletage, fetching focus on the bands that sing the story of your life, your loved ones, and the little treasures you've picked up along the way.

ring necklace

JEWELRY

INGREDIENTS
- cord or ribbon
- lots of rings

1. Gather your collection of rings. If you've come up a tad short, add a few large beads, or washers from the hardware store, to fill in. P.S.-Get creative with different colors and textures of rope and ribbon.

2. Cut the cord or ribbon to desired length and slide on the rings.

slide 'n tie it

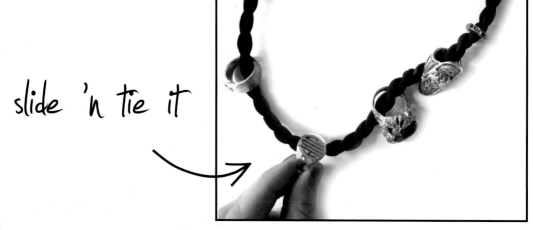

JEWELRY

Who says you need a reason to celebrate? I'm all for popping open a bottle of bubbly—on the spur of the moment or for a special occasion.

Cork, harvested from the bark of cork oaks, is a lightweight fashion heavyweight. Once used for buoys in the bay, it now lends itself graciously to nautical details on deck and below.

A natural mainstay, cork often gets a second life in bold designs and accessories. Retro and modern furniture designers use Mother Earth's material as the foundation for chairs, armoires, and lamps. In fashion, it's seen mostly during the spring and summer seasons, when it's widely incorporated into the bases of our favorite wedge heels.

Adding metallic elements to cork-based designs makes for a sought-after and stunning combination. Typically seen in hues of beige, buff, brown, camel, and tan, this raw and stylish substance is a must-have element in your accessory circuit.

Be on the lookout: Corks tend to have interesting inscriptions and graphic stampings that will help to make your staggeringly stunning pair of cork earrings pop.

cork earrings

JEWELRY

INGREDIENTS

- corks
- utility knife
- studs
- straight pins
- thin jewelry wire
- earring wires
- small beads
- pliers
- wire cutters

1. Slice two corks horizontally into thin disks.

2. Snip the straight pin to approximately 1 inch.

3. Connect the two cork pieces using the cut straight pin.

4. Wrap and twist the wire around the top cork.

5. Finish off with a bead to secure the wire.

6. Press studs directly into the cork.

7. Add the earring wire.

slice it

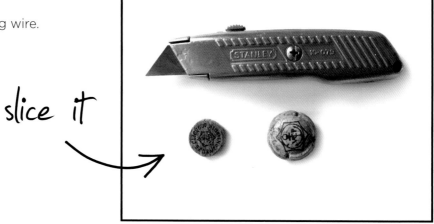

ship it

push it

wrap it

JEWELRY

twist it

bead it

stud it

JEWELRY

Fascination with the rich and famous is a guilty pleasure. We've all hankered to be a part of the cool kids' clique, whether it was New York's Upper East Side or the coveted zip code of 90210.

Perhaps you've been dreaming of the ivy-covered walls of a secret Skull and Bones–like society or an über-elite private school, where the student body sports letter jackets and school uniforms boasting their prestigious institution's patch.

Ralph Lauren, the headmaster of all things preppy, uses the runway to educate us all in present-day prep, proving that you don't need to attend class to dress as if you're seated in the front row.

Show your status and your school spirit by gluing a signifying patch onto a pair of jeans or cutoffs, or a miniskirt. Celebrate your own alma mater—or one you've always coveted—as you bring a superlative edge to your inner prep.

prep-patch necklace

JEWELRY

INGREDIENTS

- patch
- denim
- chain
- cord
- glue gun
- scissors

1. Place your patch on a piece of denim. Trace it, leaving a border. Cut two swatches.

2. Glue your patch onto one denim swatch.

3. Snip the chain into three different lengths.

4. Glue the chains and cord to the back of the patch.

5. Glue the second denim swatch onto the back of the necklace.

6. Add trim or braid elements to transform your patch into a stunning and exclusive accessory.

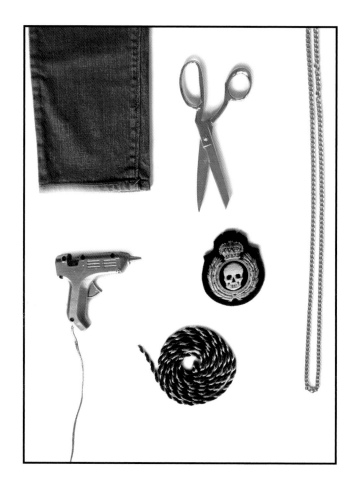

trace it

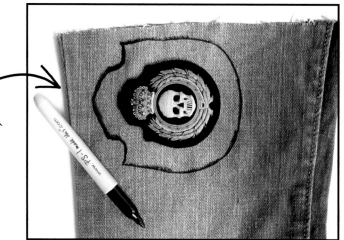

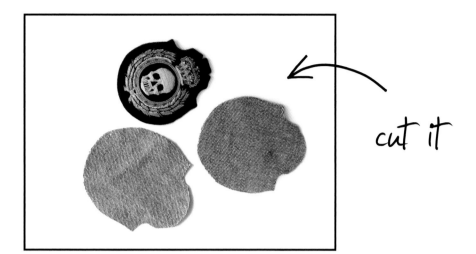

cut it

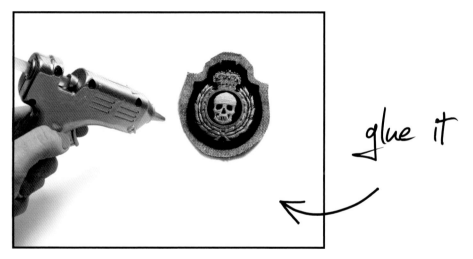

glue it

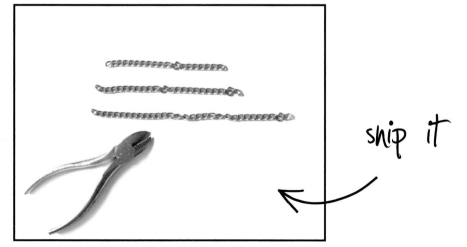

ship it

JEWELRY

chain it

cord it

cover it

lucite necklace

JEWELRY

Clear vision, clear mind, and clear focus . . . Clarity is a rarity, and we strive daily to achieve it in every way possible.

It's also the third C to look for when buying a diamond, which may be why I'm forever drawn to all things clear. See-through objects embody inspiring, sleek lightness—perfection in the most imperfect way. Translucent hues are deliciously delicate and capture our gaze. Decor essentials, such as beautiful glass bowls, light fixtures, and modern Lucite chairs, are classic, refreshing additions to any home. Fendi, Chanel, and Ports 1961 have showcased unclouded looks that pay homage to the Art Deco era, when resin jewelry and accessories were in high demand. Lucite accessories tend to be bold and oversized, which expresses a certain *je ne sais quoi* about personal style. Brave an unexpected clear creation, and it will measure up day or night.

lucite necklace

JEWELRY

INGREDIENTS
- triangle rulers
- safety pins
- chain

1. Snip the chain to the desired length.

2. Connect the triangle rulers to the chain with safety pins overlapping in the center. P.S.-Design your translucent treasure in different shades. Triangle rulers are available in pretty pink, baby blue, and yummy yellow.

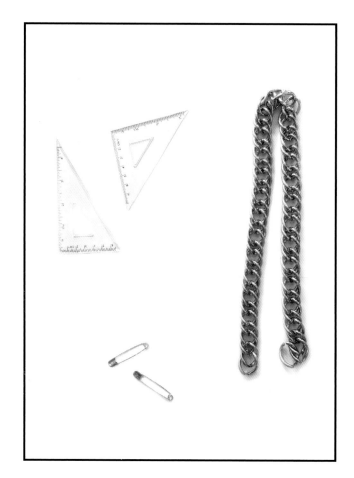

clip it

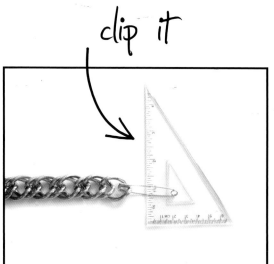

double it

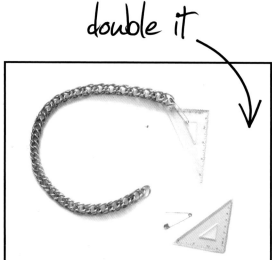

P.S.- I made this...

ACCESSORIES

ACCESSORIES

Behold, the belt! This gender-bender accessory debuted as a decorative item, first worn by men over their clothing to trim their waistlines and accentuate their buff chests.

Women took to the corset, an undergarment that allowed them to squeeze into fitted, lace-up frocks. Suction-inducing effects aside, the belt eventually broke free of strictly traditional usage, wrapping its destiny for greater glory around our midsections.

Forget about holding up your bottomhalves: For you stylish insiders, this is a band of stylish outsiders. An entire category of belting beauties stretches out before you, across seasons and styles. Varying shapes, sizes, colors, and fabrics have materialized into countless chic wardrobe additions. It's a cinch to flatter your form with a skinny belt or, for a more dramatic rig, a wider option. Curate a classy combo: Play matchmaker by pairing a current-favorite topper (or feminine pop of punch) with a belt. Bows bring happiness and a smile to our faces for all the right reasons. Belts 'n bows? Simply a match made in heaven. Take a bow and make a belt.

bow belt

ACCESSORIES

INGREDIENTS

- gorilla tape
- metallic ribbon
- velcro
- glue gun
- scissors

1. Head to the hardware store for Gorilla Tape, known as "the toughest tape on the planet," and stick two pieces sticky-side together to make a belt base. The length of the belt should be at least 3 inches longer than the circumference of your waist.

2. Fold and glue the ribbon back and forth as a bow.

3. Wrap and glue another piece of ribbon to create the bow's center.

4. Glue the ribbon bow onto the belt base.

5. Glue pieces of Velcro to the ends for an easy and cool closure, and you're in the belt business!

pull it

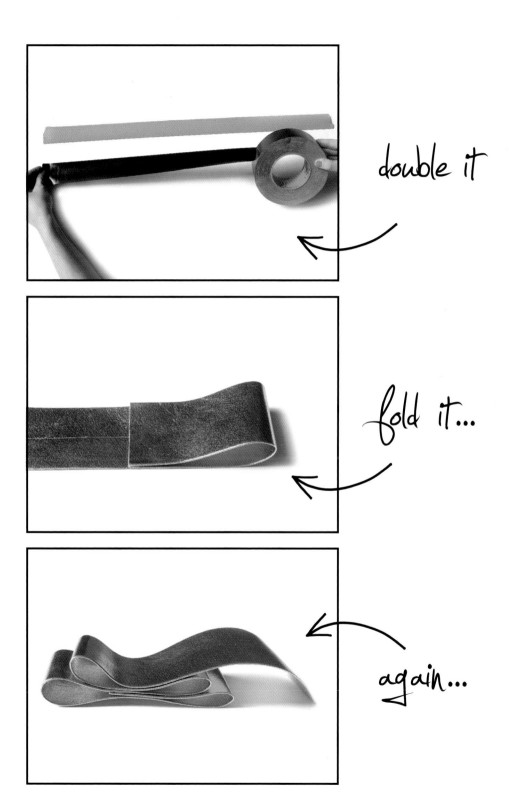

double it

fold it...

again...

bow belt

ACCESSORIES

wrap it

glue it

glue it

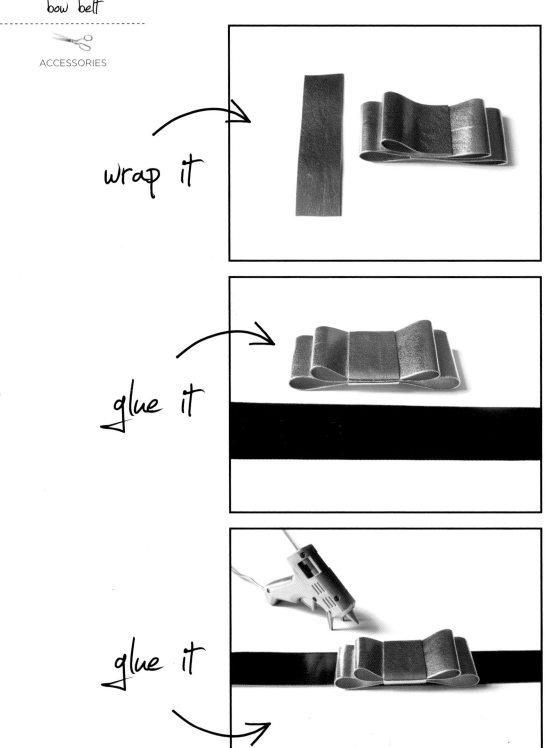

ACCESSORIES

Levi Strauss & Co. opened its doors back in the 1800s, when it introduced America to the cotton-twilled textile that has forever changed our lives and wardrobes.

Denim, the answer to all things cool, casual, and comfortable, transcends culture, style, and class, having achieved eternal-iconic status in fashion.

No matter how you rock your denim, a variety of washes, textures, finishes, and details make each piece original and *très chic*. From the farm, ranch, or railroad, real-life workers made the fabric, first used to make uniforms, an institution; however, the general public followed suit, making it work for them, too. And so the story continues.

Now, season after season, the dynamic duo of Domenico Dolce and Stefano Gabbana, who created the Italian label D&G, the younger sister of their eponymous line Dolce & Gabbana, drape damsels in distressed denims and impressive indigo-colored wear. Chloé, Marc by Marc Jacobs, Ralph Lauren, and the casual, denim-based line Madewell all have jeans as staples in their brands' genetic makeups. No matter which designer works for you, there's always a denim option to flaunt.

denim messenger purse

ACCESSORIES

INGREDIENTS

- jeans
- straight pins
- needle 'n thread
- scissors
- velcro
- chain
- wire cutters
- brooches (optional)

1. Give a new life to your denim by repurposing a pair of jeans—or shorts or a skirt! Cut off the legs of the jeans to the desired size of your bag.

2. Flip the top of the jeans inside out and pin the bottom closed.

3. Stitch across the bottom. Be sure to reinforce the ends.

4. Turn it right side out and stitch any openings together. Stick Velcro inside the waistband as the closure and stitch to reinforce.

5. Insert a chain through the belt loops, connecting the ends to complete the bag. Use a shorter length of chain for an over-the-shoulder style.

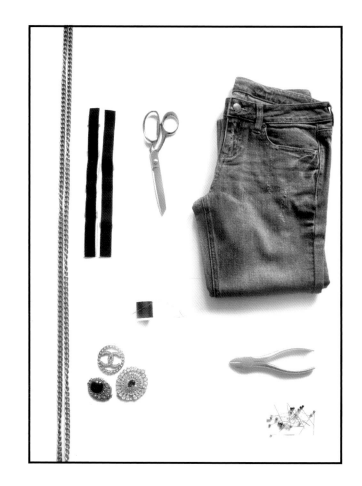

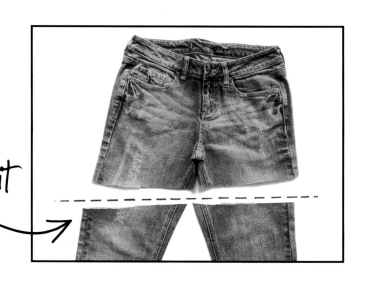

cut it

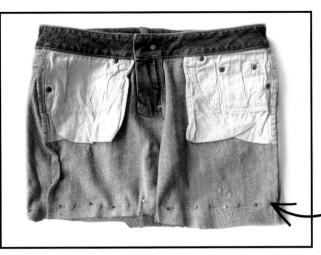

flip it 'n pin it

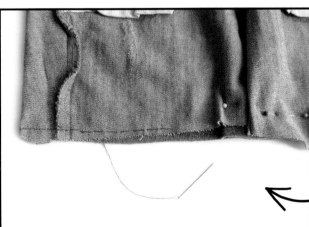

stitch it

velcro it

flip it 'n stitch it

be green,
reinvent your jeans!

ACCESSORIES

Kick up your heels in high gear as you embark on a drastic and fantastic high-heel "haul over."

Follow in the footsteps of Mr. Louboutin, Mr. Galliano, Ms. Prada, and Mr. Giuseppe Zanotti, all of whose jaw-dropping designs have elevated heels to another stiletto stratosphere. An embellished heel screams to be noticed, while keeping its lips sealed. Rhinestone details, encrusted accents, and over-the-top notions are nothing if not extraordinary.

Take a break from dripping in costume jewelry, or dazzling in sparkly dresses and tops that boast bling. Pumps and heels are a "shoe-in" when you want to step up your look. If you have a flair for the dramatic and wish to stride in style, embellish with the best of them: Re-heel your basic and boring shoes. In the spirit of the great fashion gods above, give an existing item in your closet the chance to breathe, to walk, to live life anew . . .

embellished heel

ACCESSORIES

INGREDIENTS
- pair of heels
- rhinestone strand
- glue gun
- wire cutters

1. Glue the end of the rhinestone strand at the bottom of the heel.

2. Wrap the length of the heel, using small dabs of glue to adhere.

3. Cut and glue smaller pieces to fill in any gaps. P.S.-The best bonding adhesive is either a small-nozzle glue gun or superglue.

glue it

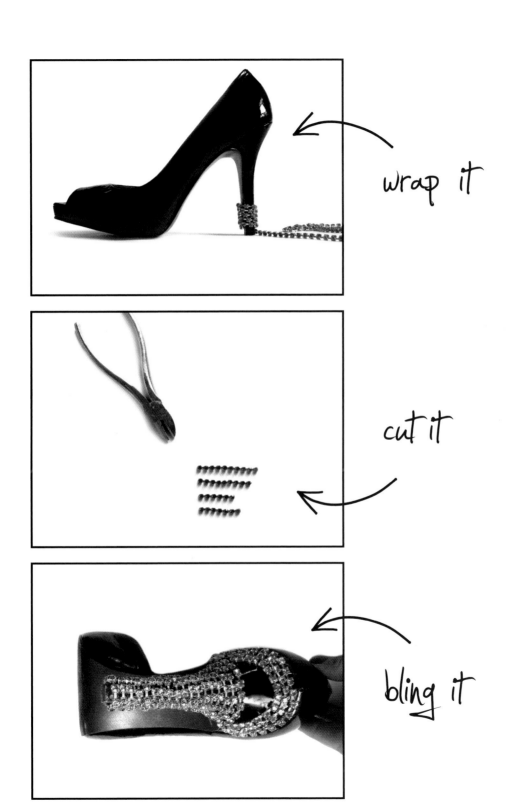

wrap it

cut it

bling it

take a walk on the wild side!

ACCESSORIES

"If you like piña coladas . . ." or getting all dressed up to enjoy them, indulge your senses with a vibrant concoction that bleeds beach chic.

Island escapes mix essential ingredients: sassy colors, juicy patterns, and flirtatious fun. The colors of the tropics bring a cheerful and positive energy—from sunup till sundown. My Chiquita Banana–loving lady, Carmen Miranda, was a celebrated samba singer and actress who whet our palates with tropical vibes, singing and dancing in her fanciful fruit-topped hat.

Designers covet tropical vacations, for which they create new fashions and accessories known as resort collections.

These colorful lines debut before the warm weather hits the cool climes and before sandy getaways are booked. Complete your look ahead of time—or live vicariously—with a "staycation" accessory: a lavish headband inspired by destinations from Palm Beach to Hawaii. Instead of tossing your tropical-drink umbrella, use it to stir up a headband!

tropical headband

ACCESSORIES

INGREDIENTS
- drink umbrellas
- scissors
- glue gun
- beads
- headband

1. Gather a supply of colorful drink umbrellas (party supply stores always carry these). Open them up and snip off the tops to remove the umbrella.

2. Cut and shape the tops into a round formation, gluing them in place.

3. Sprinkle and glue your creation with colored beads.

4. Glue the tropical designs onto a headband, or use a pin backing for a statement brooch.

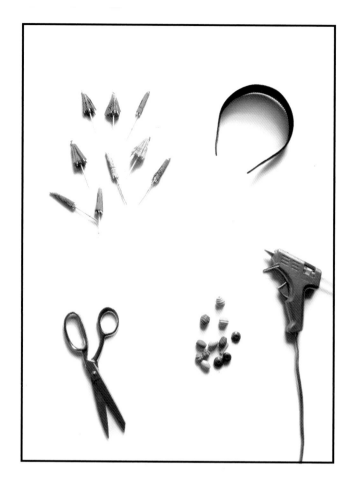

clip it

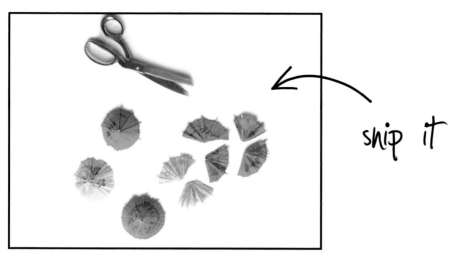

snip it

glue it

design it

happy hour turned headband!

equestrian pin

ACCESSORIES

I love ponies! Everything inspired by the four-legged beauties makes me giddy . . . especially the getups.

Classic country clubbers have been sporting sophisticated equestrian fashions for quite some time. From the posh to the preppy, this timeless look has found a soft spot in our hearts; and any way you sway, there's a designer who's trotting his or her version of it down the runway.

Hermès, Ralph Lauren, Gucci, and D&G have graciously galloped ahead of the pack with their chic interpretations. Rich leathers, bridle details, riding pants, tall boots, and brooches are staples that go beyond the stables. We look to Steven Klein for his elegant editorials and Robert Tabor for his stunning horse portraits. But nothing says a winning-equestrian look more than a first-prize pin. So saddle up: It's time to join the horsey set.

equestrian pin

ACCESSORIES

INGREDIENTS

- cupcake papers
- upholstery trim
- gems
- glue gun
- ribbon
- safety pin

1. Glue the upholstery trim onto a cupcake paper in a circular formation.

2. Gather a mix of dazzling gems. This is a great way to repurpose your broken earrings or other sparkly trinkets. Glue the cluster of gems onto the center of the lined cupcake paper.

3. Flip to the back and glue a contrasting color of upholstery trim in circular formation slightly larger than the cupcake paper. This should peek out from the front.

4. Snip two pieces of ribbon on an angle and glue to the back.

5. Attach a safety pin. Pin your prize onto your favorite blazer, handbag, blouse, or belt for added accoutrement.

glue it

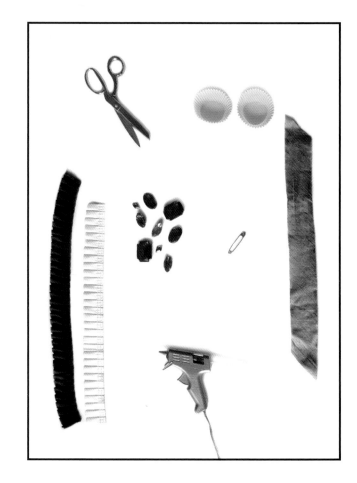

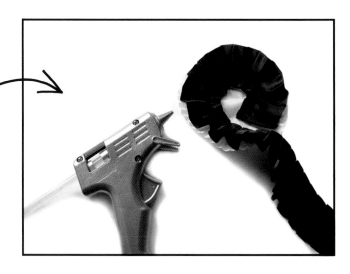

gem it

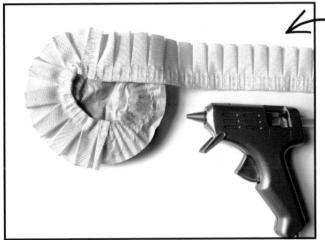

glue it

snip it

glue it

pin it

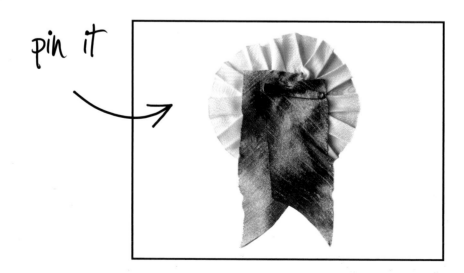

Fringe benefits are key in the game of life—and fashion.

From trusty Trojan soldiers to feminine flappers to wild Westerners, the fashion conscious throughout the ages have taken up and popularized the fringe look, which continues to sway strong. Fringe comes in all sorts of materials, ranging from suede to silk. A decorative addition to the hemline of dresses, skirts, jackets, and accessories of all kinds, dangling details will give you a swinging edge up, or the regality of rock-and-roll legend Pat Benatar, who belted out "Love Is a Battlefield" while braving the 1980s fringe trend. In the everyday world, seek inspiration from shredded paper to home accessories, such as pillows and light fixtures, their fringed edges decadent drips for the eyes to admire.

Enter the scarf, an accessory that yearns for fringing. Punch up any outfit with a fringed circle scarf. No matter what your mood, a touch of fringe will accentuate and update your look and do it with panache.

fringe scarf

ACCESSORIES

INGREDIENTS
- T-shirt
- scissors

1. Rummage through your T-shirts to find a daring print or color combination; for a cleaner, bolder look, choose a solid.

2. Cut horizontally across the shirt, just below the armholes, to create a rectangular tube.

3. Working your way around the tube, make a series of neat, vertical cuts that extend from the raw edge upward. The longer the cut, the longer the fringe will be.

4. Upon completion, tug down on each strand to elongate it. If you can't stop just yet, experiment by knotting some of the ends!

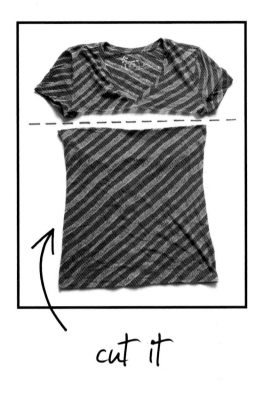

cut it

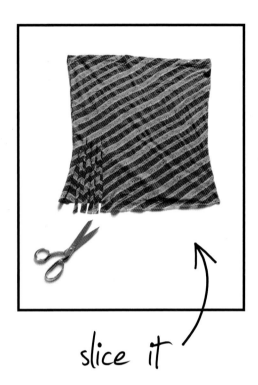

slice it

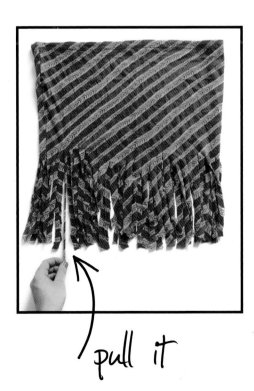

pull it

long live fringe!

gold oxford shoe

The Midas touch makes everything fabulous. The Gilded Age may be over, but the brilliant luster of golden accents still oozes opulence and decadence fit for a queen.

The golden girls of Hollywood and the gowns in which they gleam are proof one should never shy away from this jackpot hue.

Jeff Koons, an American conceptual artist, said it best (without uttering a word) with his sculpture Balloon Dog. Whether man's best friend or his best metallic ma-terial, add a dash of gold and you'll be tap dancing your way into a chic state of mind. Trade in your glass slippers for this golden-girl, slip-on favorite. The oxford shoe has evolved and is not just for dapper gents anymore. Get involved in a fierce flat fit! For winning style, go for the gold!

INGREDIENTS

- canvas sneakers
- gold spray paint
- gold sharpie paint pen
- brass fasteners
- chain
- masking tape
- wire cutters
- scissors

1. Grab a pair of sneakers hibernating in your closet or pick up a fresh pair of canvas flats. Remove the laces and cut out the tongue.

2. Stuff the shoes with paper and tape the sole.

3. Spray-paint gold, and color in the rubber sides of the soles with a metallic-gold Sharpie. (Spray paint would flake off.)

4. Add an extra karat of shine by lacing lovely chains with brass fasteners through the eyelets. (Snip if they are too long.)

5. To keep your feet and toes comfortable, *cut it* cover the brass fasteners on the underside with duct tape. P.S.-Safety first. Fasteners are sharper than they appear!

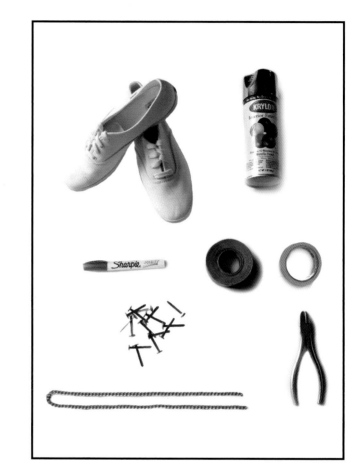

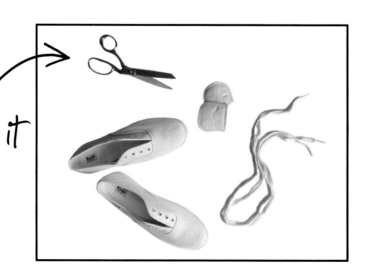

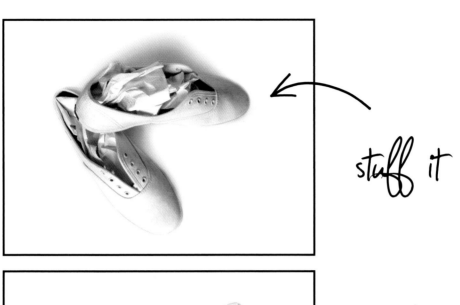

stuff it

tape it

spray it 'n paint it

ACCESSORIES

ship it

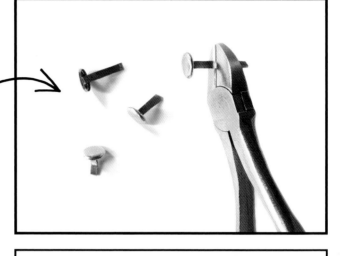

chain it

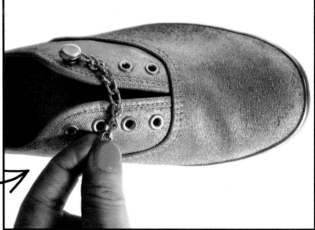

tape it

Heavy metal's never been so chic. Fashion's most prominent and coveted design houses have created iconic carryalls with heavy-metal accents that we've detected and desire.

An oversized handbag fulfills all of our toting needs. Adorned with precious materials and metallic details, handbags with shiny hardware are on a collision course, one on which style and status will meet head-on.

All hail the Birkin and Kelly bags, named respectively for the stunning actresses Jane and Grace. The first bag boasts the longest waitlist for an accessory in history, and the second was made famous by the fact that its namesake used hers to cover up her belly bump. Any way you praise or pave it, these bags, in which luxe metals are married with soft, yet substantial fabrics, are the perfect mix-ups.

Modern designs from Donna Karan, Marc Jacobs, Louis Vuitton, and Tory Burch keep us calm, helping us carry on with confidence. Protect your wallet and lip gloss while looking posh and poised. Secure your possessions with a lock, and stroll along with a "safe bet" that just may incite a riot.

We Can Do It!

hardware handbag

ACCESSORIES

INGREDIENTS

- canvas tote
- hinges
- needle 'n thread
- skinny belt
- scissors
- lock
- spray paint

1. Stitch hinges (available at your local hardware store) flat below the handles of the bag. Be sure to reinforce through the holes several times.

2. Pierce holes in the front of the bag and on the sides to set up position for the belt loop. Make sure the holes line up.

3. Get creative by spraying the lock a fun color!

4. Loop the belt through the holes and attach the lock.

stitch it

pierce it

pierce again

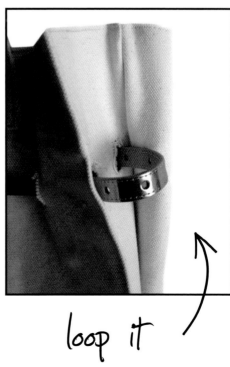

loop it

belt it

spray it

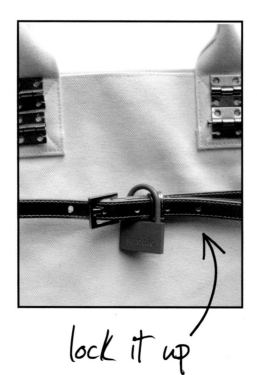

lock it up

ACCESSORIES

If you dream about running through tall grass with flowers in your hair, then you're a hippie at heart. Bohemian styles continue to be inspired by Mother Nature and the 1960s subculture.

The youth movement had a major impact on fashion, launching a trend that continues to unfold. Janis Joplin paved the way for women wanting to belt out what they believe in. Missoni, DVF, Matthew Williamson, and Tory Burch pay homage to the 1960s eclectic, Earth-loving fashions with florals, muted prints, and over-flowy, nonchalant silhouettes all their own. It's never too late to join the movement: Create a carefree headpiece inspired by the flower children, who stood their ground. Fashion favors freedom, so follow your heart and your beliefs.

INGREDIENTS

- fabric
- ribbon
- scissors
- glue gun
- needle 'n thread
- small beads

1. Round up a selection of delicate fabrics; trace and cut out large and small flower shapes.

2. Snip half-inch slits along the edges to make your flowers flutter.

3. Stack flowers and sew together to create a fuller bloom, or allow them to stand solo for a simple-and-sweet bud.

4. Fold flowers into quarters, then pinch and stitch the pointed base.

5. Finish by sewing a bead to the center.

6. Glue pieces of ribbon to each of your flower backs, and tie them, one by one, to a piece of braided ribbon.

7. Leave extra ribbon on the ends to hang down; add contrasting fabric pieces and ribbons to bring out your inner flower child.

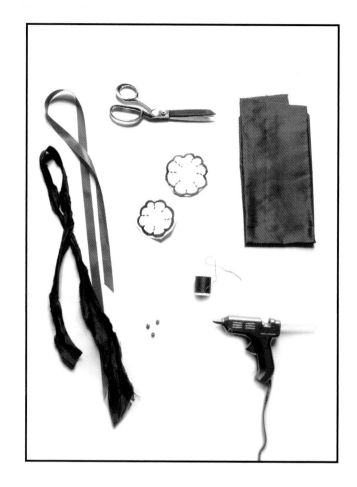

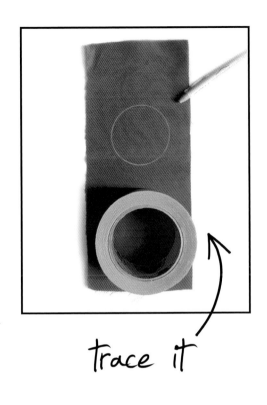

trace it

cut 'n slit it

stack it

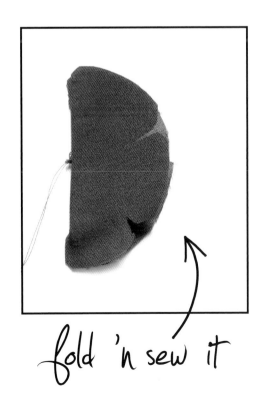

fold 'n sew it

fold again...

stitch it

sew it

bead it

glue it

position it

tie it

peace, love, and headbands...

knee-high boots

ACCESSORIES

"These boots are made for walkin'" and that's just what you'll do, thanks to Nancy Sinatra, who belted out the lyrics that we continue to embrace.

Boots elongate your "stems," with magnificent ease. Tall orders for midnight-black-leather legs and stealth stepping make me want to creep like a panther, crawl like Cat Woman, prowl for prey . . .

Betty Page was the muse for all things desirable, literally. Dubbed "the Queen of Pinups," Ms. Page frequently rocked a high boot, paired with a lusty look.

Sport knee-high boots day or night. Whether you're on the clock or out on the town, your boots—like chameleons—will adapt to and embrace the climate. Keep it classy but still evoke a hint of fierceness by pairing your boots with denim, or with dark tights and your favorite dress or skirt.

knee-high boots

ACCESSORIES

INGREDIENTS
- skinny-leg pants
- scissors

1. Find a pair of skinny-leg pants. Faux-leather or matte-vinyl pants lend themselves to a leather-like boot. Lay them on a flat surface and cut off the legs—the longer the pieces, the taller your boots will be. More is more in this case: It's good to leave the legs long; for shorter boots, you can always fold down the tops.

2. Snip a wedge to create a stirruplike opening. It will resemble a leg warmer.

3. Pair 'em with your favorite shoes. For a flat boot, wear flats; for a high-heeled boot, wear your favorite pumps.

cut it   snip it

There are some who never forget a face—and others, a name.

When given the choice, some luxury fashion houses, such as Louis Vuitton, have allowed artists, including Stephen Sprouse and Takashi Murakami, to deface their company goods in order to spread their fashionable word.

This marketing trend dates back to the days of the *Titanic*, when steamer trunks were carryalls used by the elite for their voyages around the globe. Travelers would have their initials painted onto their luggage, hatboxes, and other bags for the purpose of identification, a practice that was later adopted by savvy branders wanting to establish instant recognition of their goods. Goyard, the French luggage company established more than 150 years ago, is the Holy Grail of luxe luggage.

Contemporary status seekers slap chic racing stripes onto the sides of their carryalls, and sometimes their initials as well, for all to see. Adding a personalized touch to just about anything increases its rarity and desirability. Where will you put your style stamp? Show your stripes by "Sharpie-ing" up a bag with your signature colors. Create a pattern, add your initials, and make it say "you"—literally!

INGREDIENTS

- purse
- paint pens
- masking tape
- stencils (optional)

1. Find a fantastic bag to personalize, and gather paint pens in a range of colors.

2. Create a leopard pattern of freeform spots in a light color and outline in a dark color.

3. To make stripes, use paper or masking tape as a guide for straight lines; color them in.

4. If you don't have perfect penmanship—or guts like Van Gogh—reach for some stencils to create a personalized name or monogram!

tape it

color it

outline it

tape it...again

ACCESSORIES

stripe it

stripe it...again

stencil it

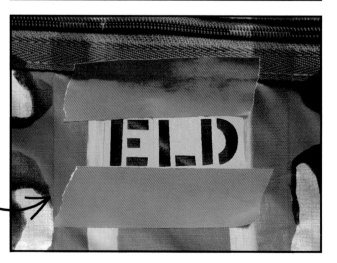

P.S.- I made this...

APPAREL

sailor's shirt

APPAREL

The great Coco Chanel once said, "When accessorizing, always take off the last thing you put on."

However, going overboard is sometimes necessary when dealing with the nautical movement, which continues to make waves both offshore and on.

Having spent much of my childhood and adulthood on and around boats, I've developed a deep love of sea-salt-inspired fashions. The casual colors associated with the nautical look are a combination of bright reds, clean whites, and all shades of blue. The inaugural ensemble was introduced by French sailors, naval gents sporting horizontal stripes and accessories to boot.

From Jacques Cousteau to Jacqueline Onassis, stylish seafarers the world over have deemed certain nautically inspired wardrobe elements must-haves. In fair or foul weather, sweet stripes mixed with gold details rank first-rate on the runways of Chanel, Michael Kors, Ralph Lauren, and Tory Burch.

Reinvent a bayside basic: the classic sailor's shirt with custom stripes and gold button details. Stay chic and sail away with style.

sailor's shirt

APPAREL

INGREDIENTS

- white T-shirt
- cardboard
- fabric spray
- masking tape
- buttons
- needle 'n thread

1. Lay the T-shirt on a flat surface and slip a piece of cardboard between the layers. Place strips of tape horizontally, leaving a thin space between each strip. This negative space will be your sailor stripe.

2. Spray in between the strips of tape with fabric spray.

3. Let dry for approximately 15 minutes before peeling off the tape.

4. Sew buttons onto the shoulder seam.

tape it

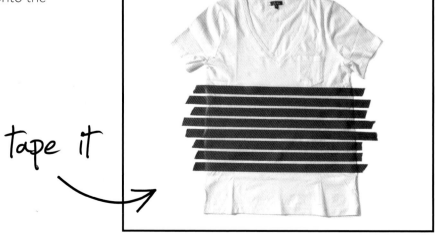

cover it

spray it

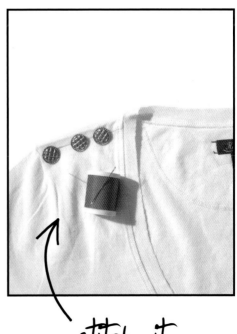

peel it

stitch it

sailor's shirt

- -

APPAREL

anchors aweigh!

faux-fur vest

Animals have beautiful, warm coats and so should we. For decades, draping oneself in fur was part of the well-to-do dress code for women of high class and sophistication.

However, faux fur is just as chic and can still look extraordinary—without having harmed any four-legged friends.

Look to fashion royalty for their fur treasures before making your faux version. America's editrix, known to most as simply "Anna," prefers sleek, classic styles, while Kate Moss frolics in long-haired, shaggy, oversized ones. Other furry accessories to

"crush" on range from an oversized fur-trapper's hat to a plush piece of flokati-fabric furniture. I, for one, strongly believe that everyone should have a luxe-fur vest, great for autumnal and blustery climates, in her wardrobe. With a quick trip to your local fabric store and your trusty scissors, you will have a wild, eye-popping, traffic-stopping piece of outerwear in just minutes.

faux-fur vest

APPAREL

INGREDIENTS

- faux-fur material
- armhole pattern
- measuring tape
- scissors
- marker

1. Spread one yard of faux-fur fabric on a flat surface and cut out a large circle.

2. Measure the width of your shoulders, map out where they will go in the circle, and cut out two narrow, evenly spaced, almond-shaped arm-holes.

3. If you want your vest to be longer in the back, place the armholes closer to the top of the circle; for an even length all the way around, place your armholes directly in the center.

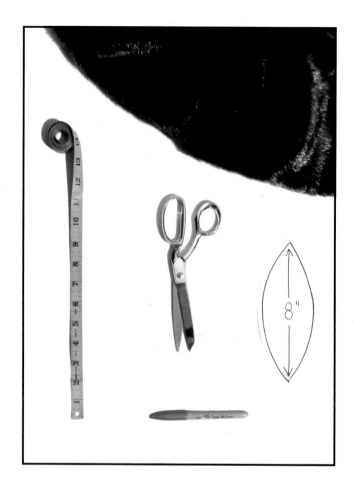

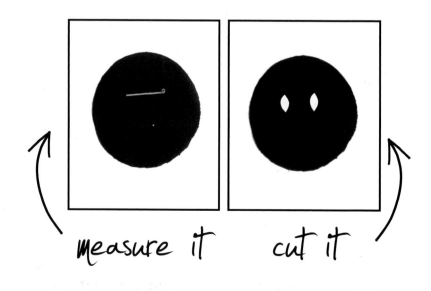

measure it   cut it

ruffle tank

APPAREL

The white ruffle, a quintessential detail that was made popular in the Edwardian era, was adopted not so long ago by style descendants we'll call the modern sophisticates.

As every thoroughly modern Millie knows, ruffles are the ultimate feminine detail. No longer just for Shakespeare's collar, ruffles have evolved, having found their way into many elegant and flirty styles. Made with a wide variety of fabrics and folds, they are creating silhouettes that are sure to ruffle some feathers.

Peek inside the studios of Lanvin, Chanel, or Mr. McQueen, and you'll see contemporary couturiers molding muslins into masterpieces festooned with ruffle accents.

ruffle tank

APPAREL

INGREDIENTS
- coffee filters
- masking tape
- scissors
- safety pins
- tank top

1. Fold and cut coffee filters to create your own fluttery layers.

2. Once your ruffles are cut, layer them on a piece of tape (sticky side up).

3. Pin the ruffle row to the tank. P.S.-Get creative—pin to dresses, skirts, and more!

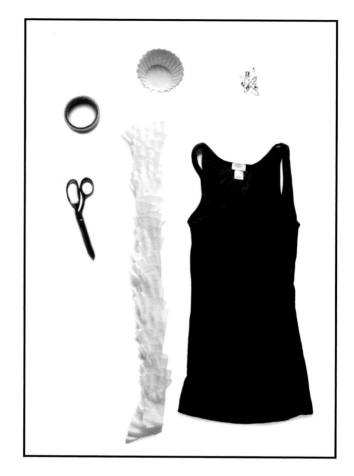

fold it

cut it

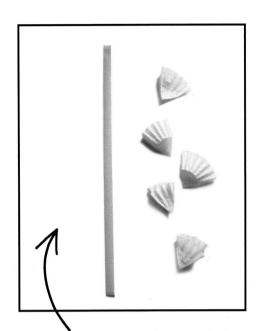

tape it... sticky side up

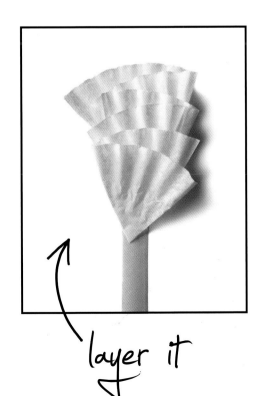

layer it

pin it

revel in those ruffles!

tuxedo pants

APPAREL

Boy meets girl. Girl falls in love with boy . . . and his pants!

The tuxedo first made its mark on men, but eventually it was embraced by female beauties begging for some boyish black tie. Yves Saint Laurent helped women embrace this menswear must-have, making the look au courant and oh, so chic!

YSL dreamed up "le smoking" (as the French call a man's tuxedo jacket) which, paired with a chic and streamlined straight pant, became the first androgynous pant-suit for ladies. Now, more than ever, de-signers draw inspiration from YSL and his stylish, rat-pack-popular pantsuit, infusing his classic silhouette with a modern sen-sibility. Stella McCartney, Ralph Lauren, Lanvin, Givenchy, Chanel, and newbie Prabal Gurung unveil new variations each season, always adding their own twists.

We all love an affair to remember, but who says you need to wait for your black-tie invite to attend? If you fancy having a leg up on this minimalist must, do a dapper update on a pair of leggings by running a wide-ribbon detail down the leg. The verti-cal accent will get you noticed, helping to elongate and slim your legs in seconds!

tuxedo pants

APPAREL

INGREDIENTS

- leggings
- decorative ribbon
- fabric glue
- needle 'n thread
- scissors

1. Choose a decorative ribbon or, depending on your personal style, a more traditional one. Cut the ribbon to the length of your leggings.

2. Beginning just below the waistband, adhere the ribbon to your leggings with a strong fabric glue.

3. Stitch as necessary for extra support.

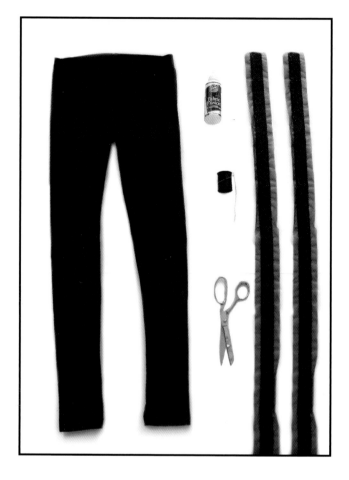

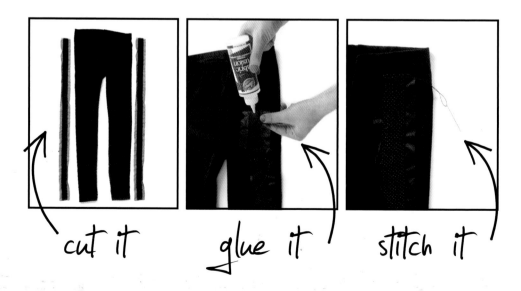

cut it   glue it   stitch it

cowl-neck vest

APPAREL

Escape with the drape and cozy up with a cowl. The cowl neck is feminine, yet strong, soft, and ever-so seductive.

Flatter your face with the style's sleepy silhouette and your whole upper half with its forgiving bias cut. Whether for a daytime date or an evening to remember, this snug style will make others want to nestle you.

From the scrumptiously folded, furry pups called shar-peis to the decorative fabrics hung as valences and curtains, inspiration for jaw-dropping draped designs may be found in unexpected places.

Donna Karan's "cozy," New York's stylish answer to the basic drape, is a versatile sweater that is what its name suggests. Other noted designers, including Diane von Furstenberg, Missoni, and Marc Jacobs, stitch fluid folds into their loose-neck dresses, blouses, and jackets. For a plunging wow, wrap yourself up in a circle scarf. For a more refined, tailored look, cinch your garment at the waist with a belt. This will draw attention to the cowl neck, heightening the drama up top while accentuating your skinny-Minnie middle below.

cowl-neck vest

INGREDIENTS

- fabric
- fabric glue
- armhole pattern
- needle 'n thread
- scissors

1. Choose from all kinds of fabric, but stay away from those that fray. For daytime, go with a lightweight cotton jersey; for evening, spice it up with the rich texture of velvet, chenille, or lamb's wool.

2. Cut your fabric into a rectangle (about a yard long).

3. Make a wide fold at the top, and "hem" it with fabric glue.

4. After the glue has dried, stitch to reinforce.

5. Measure and cut armholes that are shoulder-width apart. For a more polished look, pin the front together with your favorite brooch.

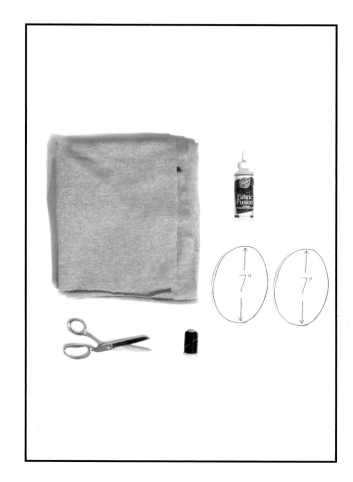

fold it

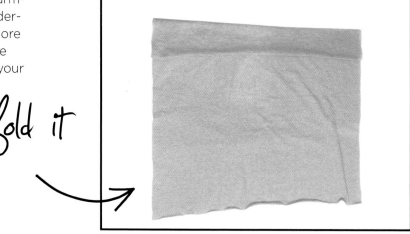

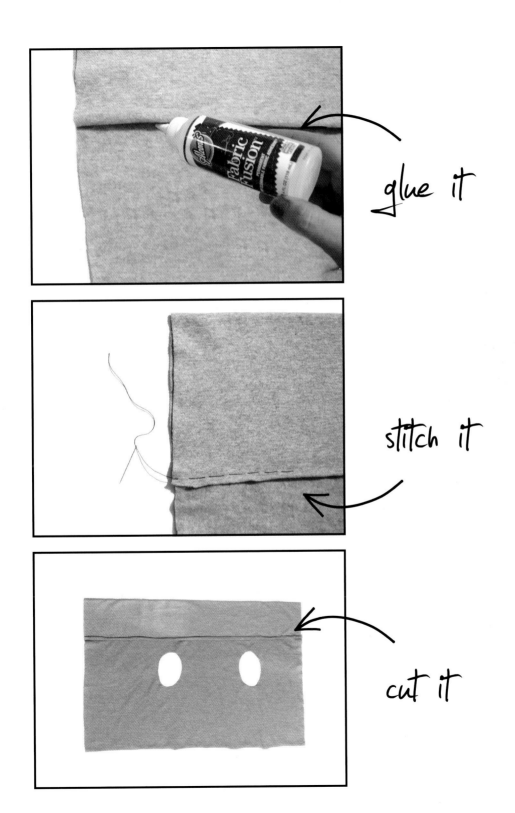

glue it

stitch it

cut it

APPAREL

start the cowl prowl

P.S.-click it...

Peruse my favorite Web sites, which are simply j'amazing! These sites provide me with an abundance of inspirational photos, features, art, designers, antiques, gossip, trends, handmade treasures, doodles, and more. Find inspiration in their content and contributors, who are always spot-on and simply get IT!

1stdibs.com

Not your grandmother's attic. Browse this decadent online marketplace for chic antiques, midcentury modern furniture, and Art Deco lighting that will leave you drooling.

designboom.com

A sleek peek inside today's modern world of architecture, art, and technology. Specializing in design acrobatics and avant-garde content that causes heads to turn and jaws to drop.

designspongeonline.com

Always spot-on for absorbing everything art, design, and interiors. A destination devoted to all things charming, picturesque, and delicate—with handmade details offering smart design solutions.

ebay.com

The world's largest online marketplace for whatever your heart desires. Scour for antique brooches, chains, decorative buttons, and festive trims to adorn your designs.

etsy.com

Buy and sell handmade DIY items that range from fashion, accessories, and apparel to art and home decor accents. Find your inner crafty-preneur and make it your business to start a business!

fashionista.com

Stylish news to scoop up daily for all things fabulous in fashion and style.

fashionweekdaily.com

Save yourself a front-row seat with free admission to Fashion Week. Keep tabs on your favorite designers and stay in the know with the Fashion Calendar for events and store openings.

polyvore.com

An online destination embraced by a global community of independent trendsetters. Create and save your own digital collages of inspiring editorial, runway, and must-have looks and items by clicking and dragging.

refinery29.com

Discover fashion's emerging talents on this site that dishes on both established and newbie designers, style news, boutique openings, insider sales, and tips from fashion industry leaders.

stylesight.com

The world's most innovative online provider of trend content combined with groundbreaking technology tools for creative professionals in the fashion, style, and design industries. This leading source allows you to efficiently and accurately search for lookbooks, runway shows, street style, art, interiors, color trends, and workshops.

style.com

Fashion's definitive Web site brings the editorial authority of *Vogue* magazine to the Internet. Style.com offers comprehensive runway coverage with photos, authoritative trend reporting, the latest social, celebrity, and fashion news, and interactive forums on every aspect of the fashion industry.

whowhatwear.com

The go-to online magazine for celebrity and runway trends, delivered daily. They answer who's wearing it, what fabulous red carpet it was on, and where you can get it.

wwd.com

Known to most as "the fashion bible," *Women's Wear Daily* serves as the voice of authority, international newswire, and agent of change for the fashion, beauty, and retail industries. WWD is delivered in both newspaper and online formats, and everyone—from retailers and designers to manufacturers and marketers—reads it daily. You should too!

P.S.-shop it...

Check out these top shops where you can swipe up the best materials for all your Designer DIY projects and everyday essentials.

ace hardware

Your neighborhood go-to resource for tools and handy items such as stencils, twine, spray paint, and more!
acehardware.com

american apparel

Known for cute and comfy apparel and accessories basics. Excellent quality, and made in the USA. **americanapparel.net**

CB2

Modern design furniture, accessories, and chic storage solutions for your home, office, or studio. Swipe up bookshelves for all your art, fashion, and design books.
cb2.com

the container store

Keep it together . . . literally. Pop by and pick up smart and chic solutions for all of your bits and bobs. Try their storage vessels for your wardrobe, jewelry, and accessories. **containerstore.com**

forever 21

This frontrunner in fast fashion specializes in apparel and accessories influenced by designer trends. A go-to for affordable and fresh merchandise to enhance, re-create, or work into DIY projects, such as belts, shoes, tops, and dresses.
forever21.com

goody

Hands down the best hair accessories to embellish. Choose snag-free elastics and comfortable headbands in a variety of colors and styles. **goody.com**

gorilla tape & glue

The world's toughest tape with a shiny sheen finish. For an accessory or heel overhaul, this is your tape! The glue is just as glorious. Find at any local hardware store or big-box retail chain.
gorillatough.com

H&M

An international destination for fast fashion and affordable pieces that are perfect for Designer DIY projects.
hm.com

home depot

The ultimate mecca for mass hardware and household items. There's nothing they don't carry! **homedepot.com**

ikea

Scandinavian modern-style furniture, accessories, and decorative items that enhance and organize any office, home, or craft room. Indulge in affordable storage options and decor such as fold-up work tables and oversized jars for gems, and check out their elegant "LACK shelves" to display art. P.S.-they sell Swedish meatballs too! **ikea.com**

Joann's fabrics

Specializes in decorative fabric and sewing supplies. A great one-stop shop for crafty goodies, with locations across the US. **joann.com**

Krylon

Spray it. Don't say it. As the spray paint leader in color innovation and inspiration, Krylon allows you to chrome, guild, matte, polish, or crack a finish fit for your personal style. Available at your local hardware store and at big-box retailers. **krylon.com**

m & j trimming

The perfect place for ribbons, trim, tassels, patches, studs, rhinestones, and embellishments galore! I refer to this as my "NYC candy store." **mjtrim.com**

Michael's

America's answer to the one-stop craft shop! Find everything from blank canvas totes to colorful glue guns and ear wires for dangling earrings. **michaels.com**

montana spray paint

Stocks an incredible variety of high-quality, brilliantly colored spray paints for artists. Easy to use, with professional looking finishes. Available at most fine art stores. **montana-spraypaint.com**

mood fabrics

A full house of haute fabrics that is to DIY for, best known as *Project Runway*'s go-to spot for lace, tulle, faux fur, and everything in between! **moodfabrics.com**

staples

All the necessary supplies required for everyday life. Make your own inspiration board from cork squares, pin up your fashion, design, and art tears with tacks, and shop till you drop for Sharpies! **staples.com**

tulip

Paint and polish your apparel and accessories. Reach for fabric paints, markers, tie-dye, paint pens, and embellishments ranging from appliqués to crystals, for fashion-forward Designer DIYs. **ilovetocreate.com**

P.S.- love it...

I bow down to all things beautiful, inspiring, and stimulating. The wide variety of stuff I "heart" spans from A to Z! P.S.-What's on your list?

A ARCHITECTURE

B BOATS

C CHANEL

D DANCE

E ETHNIC PRINTS

F FASHION MAGAZINES

G GARAGE SALES

H HORSES

I IDEAS

J JARS

K KAFTANS

L LACE

M METALLIC FINISHES

N NEON

O OCEANS

P PAPER

Q QUIRKINESS

R ROPE

S SHARPIES

T TIE-DYE

U UNIQUE TRINKETS

V VINTAGE EVERYTHING

W WOOD

X X-RAYS

Y YSL

Z ZIGZAGS

photography credits

All instructional photography by Erica Domesek, except as noted below.

Michael Fine: Front cover, 13, 19, 25, 31, 37, 43, 49, 50, 55, 59, 65, 71, 75, 77, 83, 89, 95, 101, 107, 113, 119, 125, 133, 134, 137, 143, 145, 151, 152, 155, 161–162, 165, 171; michaelfinephotography.com.

Brendan James: Back cover, 8–9; brendanjamesphotography.com.

Page 15 (clockwise from top left): Kate Spade; NASA; StyleSight (3); Popperfoto/Getty Images; Joel Stans for Tory Burch; StyleSight (3); Elfie Semotan/courtesy of Andreas Eberharter.

Page 21 (clockwise from top left): StyleSight; Richard E. Aaron/Redferns/Getty Images; StyleSight (3); Chris Nelson; Whitney Delgado; StyleSight (2); Kate Spade; StyleSight.

Page 27 (clockwise from top left): StyleSight; Chris Nelson; StyleSight (3); Kikkerdirk/Veer; StyleSight; Popperfoto/Getty Images; StyleSight.

Page 33 (clockwise from top left): Kate Spade; StyleSight (2); Business Wire/Getty Images; StyleSight (4).

Page 39 (clockwise from top left): Hugh Sitton/Getty Images; StyleSight; Ron Galella/WireImage/Getty Images; Nico Smit/Veer; StyleSight; Geoff Barrenger for Ports 1961; StyleSight (3).

Page 45 (clockwise from top left): CBS Photo Archive/Getty Images; StyleSight; Jennifer Livingston for Tory Burch; StyleSight (3); Ben Watts; Blakeley/Veer; StyleSight.

Page 51: Chris Bartlett for Tory Burch (top center); StyleSight (9) (top right).

Page 57: A. L. Whitey Schafer/John Kobal Foundation/Hulton Archive/Getty Images (center); StyleSight (10) (top right).

Page 61 (clockwise from bottom right): Elena Elisseeva/Veer; iStockphoto; StyleSight (7).

Page 67 (clockwise from top right): Ben Watts; StyleSight (3); Paramount/courtesy of Everett Collection; Chris Nelson; StyleSight (3).

Page 73 (clockwise from top left): Kate Spade; StyleSight (6); Julie Cook/Photonica/Getty Images.

Page 79 (clockwise from top right): Will Town; StyleSight; Kevin Sturman for Prabal Gurung; StyleSight (7); Hulton Archive/Getty Images.

Page 85 (from bottom right): Ben Watts; StyleSight (7); Sri, Brooklyn, NY.

Page 91 (clockwise from right center): Kate Spade; Ben Watts; StyleSight; Jody Dole/The Image Bank/Getty Images; StyleSight (6).

Page 97: (clockwise from top center): Chris Bartlett for Tory Burch; StyleSight (3); Ben Watts; David Trood/Photonica/Getty Images; Claudio Divizia/Veer; StyleSight (2); Silver Screen Collection/Hulton Archive/Getty Images.

Page 103 (clockwise from top right): Bob Tabor; Amy Risley; StyleSight; Keystone/Hulton Archive/Getty Images; StyleSight (5); Chris Nelson; Designed by Jeremy Somers.

Page 109 (clockwise from center): Nina Leen/Time & Life Pictures/Getty Images; StyleSight (2); Jennifer Livingston for Tory Burch; StyleSight (3); GAB Archive/Redferns/Getty Images; StyleSight (2).

Page 115 (clockwise from top left): Kate Spade; Denis Radovanovic/Veer; StyleSight (2); Loomis Dean/Time & Life Pictures/Getty Images; Jennifer Livingston for Tory Burch; StyleSight (4).

Page 121 (clockwise from bottom right): Tooga/The Image Bank/Getty Images; Peter Dazeley/Stone/Getty Images; StyleSight; Iofoto/Veer; StyleSight (4); Joel Stans for Tory Burch; StyleSight.

Page 127 (clockwise from top left): StyleSight; Michael Ochs Archives/Getty Images; Ben Watts (2); Jennifer Livingston for Tory Burch; Ben Watts; StyleSight (2); Whitney Delgado; iStockphoto; Keystone/Hulton Archive/Getty Images.

Page 135 (clockwise from top left): Ben Watts; StyleSight (4); iStockphoto; Terry O'Neill/Getty Images; StyleSight (2); Twentieth Century Fox/courtesy of Everett Collection; StyleSight.

Page 139 (clockwise from top left): StyleSight (2); François Dischinger for Loquita; Thanh Nguyen; StyleSight; Erica Domesek; StyleSight (2); Popperfoto/Getty Images; StyleSight.

Page 147 (clockwise from top left): Petrie Point Designs; Whitney Delgado; Ron Galella/WireImage/Getty Images; StyleSight (4); Tom Kelley/Hulton Archive/Getty Images; StyleSight; NL Shop/Veer; StyleSight.

Page 153 (clockwise from top left): StyleSight (4); Jennifer Livingston for Tory Burch; Chris Nelson; StyleSight; Arnaldo Magnani/Getty Images; StyleSight; Eric Ryan/Getty Images.

Page 157 (clockwise from top left): Geoff Barrenger for Ports 1961; StyleSight (2); John White/Veer; StyleSight (3); Ben Watts; StyleSight (2); Twentieth Century Fox/courtesy of Everett Collection.

Page 163 (clockwise from top left): StyleSight (3); Kevin Sturman for Prabal Gurung; StyleSight (3); iStockphoto (2); Soul Brother/FilmMagic/Getty Images; StyleSight; Keystone/Hulton Archive/Getty Images.

Page 167 (clockwise from top left): StyleSight; iStockphoto; StyleSight; Geoff Barrenger for Ports 1961; StyleSight (2); J. R. Eyerman/Time Life Pictures/Getty Images; Veer; StyleSight; François Dischinger for Loquita.

couldn't have

P.S.- I^made this ™ *without you*

abrams	lisa corson
amy risley	liz laffont
ben watts	michael fine
brendan james	rebecca kaplan
chris nelson	rekha luther
doug akin	samantha zipp
eleanor banco	sarah landman
jacklyn trebilcock	stylesight
jon zeiders	

EDITOR Rebecca Kaplan
DESIGNER Jill Groeber
DESIGN MANAGER Kara Strubel
PRODUCTION MANAGER Ankur Ghosh
COLLAGE DESIGNER Amy Risley

Library of Congress Cataloging-in-Publication Data

Domesek, Erica.
  P.S.; I made this— : I see it. I like it. I make it / Erica Domesek.
     p. cm.
  ISBN 978-0-8109-9603-8 (alk. paper)
  1. Clothing and dress. 2. Dress accessories. 3. Handicraft. I. Title.
  II. Title: I see it. I like it. I make it.
   TT560.D66 2010
   646.4'04--dc22

                    2010012305

Printed and bound in China
10 9 8 7 6 5 4 3 2

Abrams books are available at special discounts when purchased
in quantity for premiums and promotions as well as fundraising or
educational use. Special editions can also be created to
specification. For details, contact specialmarkets@abramsbooks.com
or the address below.

ABRAMS
THE ART OF BOOKS SINCE 1949
115 West 18th Street
New York, NY 10011
www.abramsbooks.com